SODAS JOURNAL

To Become a Masterful Problem Solver

TSG TOOLS

For

Teaching
Self-Government™

ISBN-13: 978-1492179665

ISBN-10: 1492179663

Dedication

When I first started my foster care training back in 1998, I was transformed by the SODAS. concept. I did not make up SODAS, but I feel they're an important part of my teaching self-government environment. The Utah Youth Village taught me SODAS, and they deserve credit for the problem-solving format shared in this book.

Also, a special acknowledgment to SherLynne Beach, who conceived the idea for this book and put in countless hours getting it ready for print. And finally, to my daughter Paije Peck, who helped significantly with the production process.

Table of Contents

NOTE: Write the situations for each of the completed SODAS Worksheets for easy future reference.

INTRODUCTION

This book is the companion to the SODAS PRIMER that reviews masterful problem solving. SODAS PRIMER reviews SODAS and provides examples, tips for parents, and a "What If?" game for children under 8 years old. This SODAS Journal includes a review of SODAS, practice ideas, and many blank SODAS worksheets to use in the mastery of SODAS.

For more details on how to properly use SODAS, join the Teaching Self-Government community by going to teachingselfgovernment.com where you'll find books, articles, classes, and the TSG Implementation Course All of these tools will empower you and your family to achieve greater peace and self-government.

WHY HAVE A SODAS JOURNAL?

This SODAS Journal is meant to be used, worn, written in, referred to, and even loved. It can be used by the whole family or by an individual — whatever works best for your situation.

This Journal is designed to have a way to track the learning process for each child by recording the entire SODAS experience from the situation to the solution. There may also be situations in the present that require going back to see what was decided in the past and seeing if there was a different solution or if the past solution worked for the child. It can also be fun and revealing to observe the child's growth towards self-government. Last of all, SODAS creates awareness in the family about the cause and effect of various and common situations to the family, often leading to great conversations — or even laughter!

SODAS

WHAT ARE SODAS?

SODAS is an acronym for *Situation, Options, Disadvantages* and *Advantages,* and — last of all — *Solution.* Let's explore each of these:

S: Situation

Example: "Mom said that we couldn't have a cookie until after dinner. But I took one anyway, and then I said I didn't." (Lying) — Together you and your parent recreate the situation that needs attention by using the SODAS Worksheet to see if there is any other decision you could have chosen. The parent helps the child see that there really was another choice.

O: Options

We don't ever have just one option in SODAS. Because there are many options, we usually stick to three, a combination of positive and negative ones. Parents do not give options. Rather, they can ask questions to lead the thinking (if needed). If you do the majority of the thinking, then you get the most out of the experience — which is why we do SODAS.

D: Disadvantages
A: Advantages

With your parent, list at least 3 disadvantages and 3 advantages for each option. That means you will have 9 options for advantages and 9 for disadvantages, a total of 18. You might explore more than three advantages and disadvantages, if you're thinking those things anyway.

S: Solution

The solution is to be *your* solution. You get to pick. Remember, you may have to live with the solution to help you learn how to make better choices.

On the next page is an example of how written SODAS work in this workbook. Remember, the parent always gives the situation. You think up the rest. Also, "Debrief Notes" is a place where you and your parent can write some of the discussion about the SODAS.

Example of Written SODAS

Date: _Sunday May 8, 2016_   Written by: _Porter_

Situation: _I'm at a church meeting and I feel like I'm bored sitting still._

Option #1: _Stay sitting._

Disadvantages	Advantages
1 It's boring	1 Learn something
2 I might get tired	2 I won't earn negative consequences
3 I could bother people	3 Learn to sit still

Option #2: _Go out and walk around._

Disadvantages	Advantages
1 Get in trouble	1 Get a little break
2 Get hurt or lost	2 Not bored
3 Someone has to come look for me	3 None

Option #3: _Draw pictures on my paper_

Disadvantages	Advantages
1 Might not learn things	1 It's fun, so I'm not really bored
2 Might distract people	2 Might make a cool picture
3 I won't listen to the speaker	3 Could make me happy

Solution: _Stay sitting with my family_

Debrief / Notes: _____

SODAS Ideas for Practice

Here are some ideas you can use to practice SODAS:

- You're late for school and you haven't done your chore yet.

- You didn't practice your instrument all week and at your lesson you teacher asks, "How much did you practice this piece?"

- You're angry at your friend and want to say mean things about him to others.

- You know your parents told you to come right home, but a friend wants to show you his new computer game for "just a minute."

- Your brother hits you with your doll.

- You're asked to help clean up, but you don't want to.

- You don't like what was prepared for the meal and you complain and insist on other food.

- It's bedtime, but mom and dad are busy talking on the phone and forgot what time it is.

- You have an assignment due tomorrow, and you get asked to a friend's house for a game night.

- You're hungry and you eat the food that was supposed to be for the family.

- Dad tells you to mow the lawn, but you really don't want to.

- You're at a friend's house and see something you really want. You feel an urge to take it.

- You're playing a card game with your family and you realize you can see your neighbor's cards.

- Mom tells you to clean your room, but on the way you realize you haven't seen the cat all morning and want to go looking for her.

- You're asked to feed the pets, but forget.

- Your sister took your book without asking.

- You said you would prepare a food item for a party, but you didn't have time to get it done.

- Your parents tell you that you can't go to a party and you already promised your friends you would go.

- Your family wants you to go to the canyon on a picnic, but you would rather stay at home and play computer games.

- You feel frustrated and kick the cat.

- You feel really tired, but it's time to get up in the morning.

SODAS Worksheet

Problem Solving

Date: _____ Written by: _____

Situation: _____

Option #1: _____

Disadvantages	Advantages
1	1
2	2
3	3

Option #2: _____

Disadvantages	Advantages
1	1
2	2
3	3

Option #3: _____

Disadvantages	Advantages
1	1
2	2
3	3

Solution: _____

_____

_____

Debrief / Notes: _____

_____

_____

_____

_____

_____

_____

_____

_____

_____

_____

_____

_____

SODAS Worksheet

Problem Solving

Date: _____ Written by: _____

Situation: _____

Option #1: _____

Disadvantages	Advantages
1	1
2	2
3	3

Option #2: _____

Disadvantages	Advantages
1	1
2	2
3	3

Option #3: _____

Disadvantages	Advantages
1	1
2	2
3	3

Solution: _____
_____
_____

Debrief / Notes: _____
_____
_____
_____
_____
_____
_____
_____
_____
_____
_____
_____
_____

SODAS Worksheet

Problem Solving

Date: _____ Written by: _____

Situation: _____

Option #1: _____

Disadvantages	Advantages
1	1
2	2
3	3

Option #2: _____

Disadvantages	Advantages
1	1
2	2
3	3

Option #3: _____

Disadvantages	Advantages
1	1
2	2
3	3

Solution: _____

_____

_____

Debrief / Notes: _____

_____

_____

_____

_____

_____

_____

_____

_____

_____

_____

_____

_____

_____

SODAS Worksheet
Problem Solving

Date: _____ Written by: _____

Situation: _____

Option #1: _____

Disadvantages	Advantages
1	1
2	2
3	3

Option #2: _____

Disadvantages	Advantages
1	1
2	2
3	3

Option #3: _____

Disadvantages	Advantages
1	1
2	2
3	3

Solution: _____
_____
_____

Debrief / Notes: _____
_____
_____
_____
_____
_____
_____
_____
_____
_____
_____
_____
_____

SODAS Worksheet
Problem Solving

Date: _____   Written by: _____

Situation: _____

Option #1: _____

Disadvantages	Advantages
1	1
2	2
3	3

Option #2: _____

Disadvantages	Advantages
1	1
2	2
3	3

Option #3: _____

Disadvantages	Advantages
1	1
2	2
3	3

Solution: _____
_____
_____

Debrief / Notes: _____
_____
_____
_____
_____
_____
_____
_____
_____
_____
_____
_____

SODAS Worksheet

Problem Solving

Date: _____ Written by: _____

Situation: _____

Option #1: _____

Disadvantages	Advantages
1	1
2	2
3	3

Option #2: _____

Disadvantages	Advantages
1	1
2	2
3	3

Option #3: _____

Disadvantages	Advantages
1	1
2	2
3	3

Solution: _____
_____
_____

Debrief / Notes: _____
_____
_____
_____
_____
_____
_____
_____
_____
_____
_____
_____
_____
_____
_____
_____

SODAS Worksheet

Problem Solving

Date: _____   Written by: _____

Situation: _____

Option #1: _____

Disadvantages	Advantages
1	1
2	2
3	3

Option #2: _____

Disadvantages	Advantages
1	1
2	2
3	3

Option #3: _____

Disadvantages	Advantages
1	1
2	2
3	3

Solution: _____
_____
_____

Debrief / Notes: _____
_____
_____
_____
_____
_____
_____
_____
_____
_____
_____
_____
_____
_____
_____
_____

SODAS Worksheet
Problem Solving

Date: _____   Written by: _____

Situation: _____

Option #1: _____

Disadvantages	Advantages
1	1
2	2
3	3

Option #2: _____

Disadvantages	Advantages
1	1
2	2
3	3

Option #3: _____

Disadvantages	Advantages
1	1
2	2
3	3

Solution: _____

_____

_____

Debrief / Notes: _____

_____

_____

_____

_____

_____

_____

_____

_____

_____

_____

_____

_____

_____

SODAS Worksheet

Problem Solving

Date: _____   Written by: _____

Situation: _____

Option #1: _____

Disadvantages	Advantages
1	1
2	2
3	3

Option #2: _____

Disadvantages	Advantages
1	1
2	2
3	3

Option #3: _____

Disadvantages	Advantages
1	1
2	2
3	3

Solution: _____

_____

_____

Debrief / Notes: _____

_____

_____

_____

_____

_____

_____

_____

_____

_____

_____

_____

_____

SODAS Worksheet

Problem Solving

Date: _____   Written by: _____

Situation: _____

Option #1: _____

Disadvantages	Advantages
1	1
2	2
3	3

Option #2: _____

Disadvantages	Advantages
1	1
2	2
3	3

Option #3: _____

Disadvantages	Advantages
1	1
2	2
3	3

Solution: _____
_____
_____

Debrief / Notes: _____
_____
_____
_____
_____
_____
_____
_____
_____
_____
_____
_____
_____
_____

SODAS Worksheet

Problem Solving

Date: _____ Written by: _____

Situation: _____

Option #1: _____

Disadvantages	Advantages
1	1
2	2
3	3

Option #2: _____

Disadvantages	Advantages
1	1
2	2
3	3

Option #3: _____

Disadvantages	Advantages
1	1
2	2
3	3

Solution: _____

_____

_____

Debrief / Notes: _____

_____

_____

_____

_____

_____

_____

_____

_____

_____

_____

_____

_____

SODAS Worksheet

Problem Solving

Date: _____ Written by: _____

Situation: _____

Option #1: _____

Disadvantages	Advantages
1	1
2	2
3	3

Option #2: _____

Disadvantages	Advantages
1	1
2	2
3	3

Option #3: _____

Disadvantages	Advantages
1	1
2	2
3	3

Solution: _____
_____
_____

Debrief / Notes: _____
_____
_____
_____
_____
_____
_____
_____
_____
_____
_____
_____
_____
_____

SODAS Worksheet

Problem Solving

Date: _____ Written by: _____

Situation: _____

Option #1: _____

Disadvantages	Advantages
1	1
2	2
3	3

Option #2: _____

Disadvantages	Advantages
1	1
2	2
3	3

Option #3: _____

Disadvantages	Advantages
1	1
2	2
3	3

Solution: _____
_____
_____

Debrief / Notes: _____
_____
_____
_____
_____
_____
_____
_____
_____
_____
_____
_____
_____

SODAS Worksheet

Problem Solving

Date: _____ Written by: _____

Situation: _____

Option #1: _____

Disadvantages	Advantages
1	1
2	2
3	3

Option #2: _____

Disadvantages	Advantages
1	1
2	2
3	3

Option #3: _____

Disadvantages	Advantages
1	1
2	2
3	3

Solution: _____
_____
_____

Debrief / Notes: _____
_____
_____
_____
_____
_____
_____
_____
_____
_____
_____
_____
_____
_____

SODAS Worksheet

Problem Solving

Date: _____   Written by: _____

Situation: _____

Option #1: _____

Disadvantages	Advantages
1	1
2	2
3	3

Option #2: _____

Disadvantages	Advantages
1	1
2	2
3	3

Option #3: _____

Disadvantages	Advantages
1	1
2	2
3	3

Solution: _____
_____
_____

Debrief / Notes: _____
_____
_____
_____
_____
_____
_____
_____
_____
_____
_____
_____
_____
_____

SODAS Worksheet

Problem Solving

Date: _____ Written by: _____

Situation: _____

Option #1: _____

Disadvantages	Advantages
1	1
2	2
3	3

Option #2: _____

Disadvantages	Advantages
1	1
2	2
3	3

Option #3: _____

Disadvantages	Advantages
1	1
2	2
3	3

Solution: _____
_____
_____

Debrief / Notes: _____
_____
_____
_____
_____
_____
_____
_____
_____
_____
_____
_____
_____

SODAS Worksheet

Problem Solving

Date: _____ Written by: _____

Situation: _____

Option #1: _____

Disadvantages	Advantages
1	1
2	2
3	3

Option #2: _____

Disadvantages	Advantages
1	1
2	2
3	3

Option #3: _____

Disadvantages	Advantages
1	1
2	2
3	3

Solution: _____
_____
_____

Debrief / Notes: _____
_____
_____
_____
_____
_____
_____
_____
_____
_____
_____
_____
_____
_____
_____

SODAS Worksheet
Problem Solving

Date: _____   Written by: _____

Situation: _____

Option #1: _____

Disadvantages	Advantages
1	1
2	2
3	3

Option #2: _____

Disadvantages	Advantages
1	1
2	2
3	3

Option #3: _____

Disadvantages	Advantages
1	1
2	2
3	3

Solution: _____
_____
_____

Debrief / Notes: _____
_____
_____
_____
_____
_____
_____
_____
_____
_____
_____
_____
_____
_____

SODAS Worksheet
Problem Solving

Date: _____   Written by: _____

Situation: _____

Option #1: _____

Disadvantages	Advantages
1	1
2	2
3	3

Option #2: _____

Disadvantages	Advantages
1	1
2	2
3	3

Option #3: _____

Disadvantages	Advantages
1	1
2	2
3	3

Solution: _____

_____

_____

Debrief / Notes: _____

_____

_____

_____

_____

_____

_____

_____

_____

_____

_____

_____

_____

SODAS Worksheet

Problem Solving

Date: _____   Written by: _____

Situation: _____

Option #1: _____

Disadvantages	Advantages
1	1
2	2
3	3

Option #2: _____

Disadvantages	Advantages
1	1
2	2
3	3

Option #3: _____

Disadvantages	Advantages
1	1
2	2
3	3

Solution: _____
_____
_____
_____

Debrief / Notes: _____
_____
_____
_____
_____
_____
_____
_____
_____
_____
_____
_____
_____
_____

SODAS Worksheet

Problem Solving

Date: _____   Written by: _____

Situation: _____

Option #1: _____

Disadvantages	Advantages
1	1
2	2
3	3

Option #2: _____

Disadvantages	Advantages
1	1
2	2
3	3

Option #3: _____

Disadvantages	Advantages
1	1
2	2
3	3

Solution: _____
_____
_____

Debrief / Notes: _____
_____
_____
_____
_____
_____
_____
_____
_____
_____
_____
_____
_____

SODAS Worksheet
Problem Solving

Date: _____ Written by: _____

Situation: _____

Option #1: _____

Disadvantages	Advantages
1	1
2	2
3	3

Option #2: _____

Disadvantages	Advantages
1	1
2	2
3	3

Option #3: _____

Disadvantages	Advantages
1	1
2	2
3	3

Solution: _____
_____
_____

Debrief / Notes: _____

_____

_____

_____

_____

_____

_____

_____

_____

_____

_____

_____

_____

_____

SODAS Worksheet
Problem Solving

Date: _____   Written by: _____

Situation: _____

Option #1: _____

Disadvantages	Advantages
1	1
2	2
3	3

Option #2: _____

Disadvantages	Advantages
1	1
2	2
3	3

Option #3: _____

Disadvantages	Advantages
1	1
2	2
3	3

Solution: _____
_____
_____

Debrief / Notes: _____
_____
_____
_____
_____
_____
_____
_____
_____
_____
_____
_____

SODAS Worksheet

Problem Solving

Date: _____   Written by: _____

Situation: _____

Option #1: _____

Disadvantages	Advantages
1	1
2	2
3	3

Option #2: _____

Disadvantages	Advantages
1	1
2	2
3	3

Option #3: _____

Disadvantages	Advantages
1	1
2	2
3	3

Solution: _____
_____
_____

Debrief / Notes: _____
_____
_____
_____
_____
_____
_____
_____
_____
_____
_____
_____
_____

SODAS Worksheet

Problem Solving

Date: _____   Written by: _____

Situation: _____

Option #1: _____

Disadvantages	Advantages
1	1
2	2
3	3

Option #2: _____

Disadvantages	Advantages
1	1
2	2
3	3

Option #3: _____

Disadvantages	Advantages
1	1
2	2
3	3

Solution: _____

_____

_____

Debrief / Notes: _____

_____

_____

_____

_____

_____

_____

_____

_____

_____

_____

_____

_____

SODAS Worksheet
Problem Solving

Date: _____ Written by: _____

Situation: _____

Option #1: _____

Disadvantages	Advantages
1	1
2	2
3	3

Option #2: _____

Disadvantages	Advantages
1	1
2	2
3	3

Option #3: _____

Disadvantages	Advantages
1	1
2	2
3	3

Solution: _____
_____
_____

Debrief / Notes: _____
_____
_____
_____
_____
_____
_____
_____
_____
_____
_____
_____
_____
_____
_____

SODAS Worksheet

Problem Solving

Date: _____ Written by: _____

Situation: _____

Option #1: _____

Disadvantages	Advantages
1	1
2	2
3	3

Option #2: _____

Disadvantages	Advantages
1	1
2	2
3	3

Option #3: _____

Disadvantages	Advantages
1	1
2	2
3	3

Solution: _____
_____
_____

Debrief / Notes: _____
_____
_____
_____
_____
_____
_____
_____
_____
_____
_____
_____
_____
_____
_____

SODAS Worksheet
Problem Solving

Date: _____ Written by: _____

Situation: _____

Option #1: _____

Disadvantages	Advantages
1	1
2	2
3	3

Option #2: _____

Disadvantages	Advantages
1	1
2	2
3	3

Option #3: _____

Disadvantages	Advantages
1	1
2	2
3	3

Solution: _____
_____
_____

Debrief / Notes: _____
_____
_____
_____
_____
_____
_____
_____
_____
_____
_____
_____
_____
_____

SODAS Worksheet
Problem Solving

Date: _____   Written by: _____

Situation: _____

Option #1: _____

Disadvantages	Advantages
1	1
2	2
3	3

Option #2: _____

Disadvantages	Advantages
1	1
2	2
3	3

Option #3: _____

Disadvantages	Advantages
1	1
2	2
3	3

Solution: _____
_____
_____

Debrief / Notes: _____
_____
_____
_____
_____
_____
_____
_____
_____
_____
_____
_____
_____
_____

SODAS Worksheet

Problem Solving

Date: _____   Written by: _____

Situation: _____

Option #1: _____

Disadvantages	Advantages
1	1
2	2
3	3

Option #2: _____

Disadvantages	Advantages
1	1
2	2
3	3

Option #3: _____

Disadvantages	Advantages
1	1
2	2
3	3

Solution: _____
_____
_____

Debrief / Notes: _____
_____
_____
_____
_____
_____
_____
_____
_____
_____
_____
_____
_____

SODAS Worksheet

Problem Solving

Date: _____   Written by: _____

Situation: _____

Option #1: _____

Disadvantages	Advantages
1	1
2	2
3	3

Option #2: _____

Disadvantages	Advantages
1	1
2	2
3	3

Option #3: _____

Disadvantages	Advantages
1	1
2	2
3	3

Solution: _____

_____

_____

Debrief / Notes: _____

_____

_____

_____

_____

_____

_____

_____

_____

_____

_____

_____

_____

SODAS Worksheet

Problem Solving

Date: _____   Written by: _____

Situation: _____

Option #1: _____

Disadvantages	Advantages
1	1
2	2
3	3

Option #2: _____

Disadvantages	Advantages
1	1
2	2
3	3

Option #3: _____

Disadvantages	Advantages
1	1
2	2
3	3

Solution: _____
_____
_____

Debrief / Notes: _____
_____
_____
_____
_____
_____
_____
_____
_____
_____
_____
_____
_____

SODAS Worksheet

Problem Solving

Date: _____ Written by: _____

Situation: _____

Option #1: _____

Disadvantages	Advantages
1	1
2	2
3	3

Option #2: _____

Disadvantages	Advantages
1	1
2	2
3	3

Option #3: _____

Disadvantages	Advantages
1	1
2	2
3	3

Solution: _____

_____

_____

Debrief / Notes: _____

_____

_____

_____

_____

_____

_____

_____

_____

_____

_____

_____

_____

_____

_____

SODAS Worksheet

Problem Solving

Date: _____   Written by: _____

Situation: _____

Option #1: _____

Disadvantages	Advantages
1	1
2	2
3	3

Option #2: _____

Disadvantages	Advantages
1	1
2	2
3	3

Option #3: _____

Disadvantages	Advantages
1	1
2	2
3	3

Solution: _____
_____
_____

Debrief / Notes: _____
_____
_____
_____
_____
_____
_____
_____
_____
_____
_____
_____
_____

SODAS Worksheet
Problem Solving

Date: _____   Written by: _____

Situation: _____

Option #1: _____

Disadvantages	Advantages
1	1
2	2
3	3

Option #2: _____

Disadvantages	Advantages
1	1
2	2
3	3

Option #3: _____

Disadvantages	Advantages
1	1
2	2
3	3

Solution: _____

_____

_____

Debrief / Notes: _____

_____

_____

_____

_____

_____

_____

_____

_____

_____

_____

_____

_____

_____

SODAS Worksheet
Problem Solving

Date: _____   Written by: _____

Situation: _____

Option #1: _____

Disadvantages	Advantages
1	1
2	2
3	3

Option #2: _____

Disadvantages	Advantages
1	1
2	2
3	3

Option #3: _____

Disadvantages	Advantages
1	1
2	2
3	3

Solution: _____

_____

_____

_____

Debrief / Notes: _____

_____

_____

_____

_____

_____

_____

_____

_____

_____

_____

_____

_____

_____

SODAS Worksheet
Problem Solving

Date: _____ Written by: _____

Situation: _____

Option #1: _____

Disadvantages	Advantages
1	1
2	2
3	3

Option #2: _____

Disadvantages	Advantages
1	1
2	2
3	3

Option #3: _____

Disadvantages	Advantages
1	1
2	2
3	3

Solution: _____
_____
_____

Debrief / Notes: _____
_____
_____
_____
_____
_____
_____
_____
_____
_____
_____
_____
_____

SODAS Worksheet

Problem Solving

Date: _____ Written by: _____

Situation: _____

Option #1: _____

Disadvantages	Advantages
1	1
2	2
3	3

Option #2: _____

Disadvantages	Advantages
1	1
2	2
3	3

Option #3: _____

Disadvantages	Advantages
1	1
2	2
3	3

Solution: _____

_____

_____

Debrief / Notes: _____

_____

_____

_____

_____

_____

_____

_____

_____

_____

_____

_____

_____

SODAS Worksheet

Problem Solving

Date: _____   Written by: _____

Situation: _____

Option #1: _____

Disadvantages	Advantages
1	1
2	2
3	3

Option #2: _____

Disadvantages	Advantages
1	1
2	2
3	3

Option #3: _____

Disadvantages	Advantages
1	1
2	2
3	3

Solution: _____

_____

_____

Debrief / Notes: _____

_____

_____

_____

_____

_____

_____

_____

_____

_____

_____

_____

_____

_____

SODAS Worksheet
Problem Solving

Date: _____   Written by: _____

Situation: _____

Option #1: _____

Disadvantages	Advantages
1	1
2	2
3	3

Option #2: _____

Disadvantages	Advantages
1	1
2	2
3	3

Option #3: _____

Disadvantages	Advantages
1	1
2	2
3	3

Solution: _____
_____
_____

Debrief / Notes: _____
_____
_____
_____
_____
_____
_____
_____
_____
_____
_____
_____
_____

SODAS Worksheet
Problem Solving

Date: _____ Written by: _____

Situation: _____

Option #1: _____

Disadvantages	Advantages
1	1
2	2
3	3

Option #2: _____

Disadvantages	Advantages
1	1
2	2
3	3

Option #3: _____

Disadvantages	Advantages
1	1
2	2
3	3

Solution: _____
_____
_____

Debrief / Notes: _____
_____
_____
_____
_____
_____
_____
_____
_____
_____
_____
_____
_____
_____

SODAS Worksheet

Problem Solving

Date: _____ Written by: _____

Situation: _____

Option #1: _____

Disadvantages	Advantages
1	1
2	2
3	3

Option #2: _____

Disadvantages	Advantages
1	1
2	2
3	3

Option #3: _____

Disadvantages	Advantages
1	1
2	2
3	3

Solution: _____
_____
_____

Debrief / Notes: _____
_____
_____
_____
_____
_____
_____
_____
_____
_____
_____
_____
_____
_____
_____

SODAS Worksheet
Problem Solving

Date: _____   Written by: _____

Situation: _____

Option #1: _____

Disadvantages	Advantages
1	1
2	2
3	3

Option #2: _____

Disadvantages	Advantages
1	1
2	2
3	3

Option #3: _____

Disadvantages	Advantages
1	1
2	2
3	3

Solution: _____

_____

_____

Debrief / Notes: _____

_____

_____

_____

_____

_____

_____

_____

_____

_____

_____

_____

_____

SODAS Worksheet
Problem Solving

Date: _____   Written by: _____

Situation: _____

Option #1: _____

Disadvantages	Advantages
1	1
2	2
3	3

Option #2: _____

Disadvantages	Advantages
1	1
2	2
3	3

Option #3: _____

Disadvantages	Advantages
1	1
2	2
3	3

Solution: _____
_____
_____

Debrief / Notes: _____
_____
_____
_____
_____
_____
_____
_____
_____
_____
_____
_____
_____
_____

SODAS Worksheet

Problem Solving

Date: _____ Written by: _____

Situation: _____

Option #1: _____

Disadvantages	Advantages
1	1
2	2
3	3

Option #2: _____

Disadvantages	Advantages
1	1
2	2
3	3

Option #3: _____

Disadvantages	Advantages
1	1
2	2
3	3

Solution: _____
_____
_____
_____

Debrief / Notes: _____
_____
_____
_____
_____
_____
_____
_____
_____
_____
_____
_____
_____
_____

SODAS Worksheet

Problem Solving

Date: _____   Written by: _____

Situation: _____

Option #1: _____

Disadvantages	Advantages
1	1
2	2
3	3

Option #2: _____

Disadvantages	Advantages
1	1
2	2
3	3

Option #3: _____

Disadvantages	Advantages
1	1
2	2
3	3

Solution: _____
_____
_____

Debrief / Notes: _____
_____
_____
_____
_____
_____
_____
_____
_____
_____
_____
_____
_____

SODAS Worksheet
Problem Solving

Date: _____   Written by: _____

Situation: _____

Option #1: _____

Disadvantages	Advantages
1	1
2	2
3	3

Option #2: _____

Disadvantages	Advantages
1	1
2	2
3	3

Option #3: _____

Disadvantages	Advantages
1	1
2	2
3	3

Solution: _____

_____

_____

Debrief / Notes: _____

_____

_____

_____

_____

_____

_____

_____

_____

_____

_____

_____

SODAS Worksheet
Problem Solving

Date: _____ Written by: _____

Situation: _____

Option #1: _____

Disadvantages	Advantages
1	1
2	2
3	3

Option #2: _____

Disadvantages	Advantages
1	1
2	2
3	3

Option #3: _____

Disadvantages	Advantages
1	1
2	2
3	3

Solution: _____

_____

_____

Debrief / Notes: _____

_____

_____

_____

_____

_____

_____

_____

_____

_____

_____

_____

SODAS Worksheet
Problem Solving

Date: _____   Written by: _____

Situation: _____

Option #1: _____

Disadvantages	Advantages
1	1
2	2
3	3

Option #2: _____

Disadvantages	Advantages
1	1
2	2
3	3

Option #3: _____

Disadvantages	Advantages
1	1
2	2
3	3

Solution: _____

_____

_____

Debrief / Notes: _____

_____

_____

_____

_____

_____

_____

_____

_____

_____

_____

_____

_____

_____

SODAS Worksheet
Problem Solving

Date: _____   Written by: _____

Situation: _____

Option #1: _____

Disadvantages	Advantages
1	1
2	2
3	3

Option #2: _____

Disadvantages	Advantages
1	1
2	2
3	3

Option #3: _____

Disadvantages	Advantages
1	1
2	2
3	3

Solution: _____
_____
_____

Debrief / Notes: _____
_____
_____
_____
_____
_____
_____
_____
_____
_____
_____
_____
_____
_____

SODAS Worksheet
Problem Solving

Date: _____   Written by: _____

Situation: _____

Option #1: _____

Disadvantages	Advantages
1	1
2	2
3	3

Option #2: _____

Disadvantages	Advantages
1	1
2	2
3	3

Option #3: _____

Disadvantages	Advantages
1	1
2	2
3	3

Solution: _____
_____
_____
_____

Debrief / Notes: _____
_____
_____
_____
_____
_____
_____
_____
_____
_____
_____
_____
_____
_____
_____
_____
_____

SODAS Worksheet

Problem Solving

Date: _____   Written by: _____

Situation: _____

Option #1: _____

Disadvantages	Advantages
1	1
2	2
3	3

Option #2: _____

Disadvantages	Advantages
1	1
2	2
3	3

Option #3: _____

Disadvantages	Advantages
1	1
2	2
3	3

Solution: _____

_____

_____

Debrief / Notes: _____

_____

_____

_____

_____

_____

_____

_____

_____

_____

_____

_____

_____

SODAS Worksheet

Problem Solving

Date: _____   Written by: _____

Situation: _____

Option #1: _____

Disadvantages	Advantages
1	1
2	2
3	3

Option #2: _____

Disadvantages	Advantages
1	1
2	2
3	3

Option #3: _____

Disadvantages	Advantages
1	1
2	2
3	3

Solution: _____

_____

_____

Debrief / Notes: _____

SODAS Worksheet

Problem Solving

Date: _____   Written by: _____

Situation: _____

Option #1: _____

Disadvantages	Advantages
1	1
2	2
3	3

Option #2: _____

Disadvantages	Advantages
1	1
2	2
3	3

Option #3: _____

Disadvantages	Advantages
1	1
2	2
3	3

Solution: _____
_____
_____
_____

Debrief / Notes: _____
_____
_____
_____
_____
_____
_____
_____
_____
_____
_____
_____
_____

SODAS Worksheet

Problem Solving

Date: _____ Written by: _____

Situation: _____

Option #1: _____

Disadvantages	Advantages
1	1
2	2
3	3

Option #2: _____

Disadvantages	Advantages
1	1
2	2
3	3

Option #3: _____

Disadvantages	Advantages
1	1
2	2
3	3

Solution: _____
_____
_____

Debrief / Notes: _____
_____
_____
_____
_____
_____
_____
_____
_____
_____
_____

SODAS Worksheet

Problem Solving

Date: _____ Written by: _____

Situation: _____

Option #1: _____

Disadvantages	Advantages
1	1
2	2
3	3

Option #2: _____

Disadvantages	Advantages
1	1
2	2
3	3

Option #3: _____

Disadvantages	Advantages
1	1
2	2
3	3

Solution: _____

_____

_____

Debrief / Notes: _____

_____

_____

_____

_____

_____

_____

_____

_____

_____

_____

_____

_____

_____

_____

SODAS Worksheet

Problem Solving

Date: _____ Written by: _____

Situation: _____

Option #1: _____

Disadvantages	Advantages
1	1
2	2
3	3

Option #2: _____

Disadvantages	Advantages
1	1
2	2
3	3

Option #3: _____

Disadvantages	Advantages
1	1
2	2
3	3

Solution: _____
_____
_____

Debrief / Notes: _____
_____
_____
_____
_____
_____
_____
_____
_____
_____
_____
_____
_____

SODAS Worksheet

Problem Solving

Date: _____ Written by: _____

Situation: _____

Option #1: _____

Disadvantages	Advantages
1	1
2	2
3	3

Option #2: _____

Disadvantages	Advantages
1	1
2	2
3	3

Option #3: _____

Disadvantages	Advantages
1	1
2	2
3	3

Solution: _____

_____

_____

Debrief / Notes: _____

_____

_____

_____

_____

_____

_____

_____

_____

_____

_____

_____

_____

SODAS Worksheet

Problem Solving

Date: _____   Written by: _____

Situation: _____

Option #1: _____

Disadvantages	Advantages
1	1
2	2
3	3

Option #2: _____

Disadvantages	Advantages
1	1
2	2
3	3

Option #3: _____

Disadvantages	Advantages
1	1
2	2
3	3

Solution: _____

_____

_____

Debrief / Notes: _____

_____

_____

_____

_____

_____

_____

_____

_____

_____

_____

_____

_____

SODAS Worksheet
Problem Solving

Date: _____   Written by: _____

Situation: _____

Option #1: _____

Disadvantages	Advantages
1	1
2	2
3	3

Option #2: _____

Disadvantages	Advantages
1	1
2	2
3	3

Option #3: _____

Disadvantages	Advantages
1	1
2	2
3	3

Solution: _____

_____

_____

Debrief / Notes: _____

_____

_____

_____

_____

_____

_____

_____

_____

_____

_____

_____

_____

_____

_____

SODAS Worksheet

Problem Solving

Date: _____ Written by: _____

Situation: _____

Option #1: _____

Disadvantages	Advantages
1	1
2	2
3	3

Option #2: _____

Disadvantages	Advantages
1	1
2	2
3	3

Option #3: _____

Disadvantages	Advantages
1	1
2	2
3	3

Solution: _____
_____
_____

Debrief / Notes: _____
_____
_____
_____
_____
_____
_____
_____
_____
_____
_____
_____
_____

SODAS Worksheet
Problem Solving

Date: _____   Written by: _____

Situation: _____

Option #1: _____

Disadvantages	Advantages
1	1
2	2
3	3

Option #2: _____

Disadvantages	Advantages
1	1
2	2
3	3

Option #3: _____

Disadvantages	Advantages
1	1
2	2
3	3

Solution: _____

_____

_____

Debrief / Notes: _____

_____

_____

_____

_____

_____

_____

_____

_____

_____

_____

_____

_____

SODAS Worksheet
Problem Solving

Date: _____   Written by: _____

Situation: _____

Option #1: _____

Disadvantages	Advantages
1	1
2	2
3	3

Option #2: _____

Disadvantages	Advantages
1	1
2	2
3	3

Option #3: _____

Disadvantages	Advantages
1	1
2	2
3	3

Solution: _____
_____
_____

Debrief / Notes: _____
_____
_____
_____
_____
_____
_____
_____
_____
_____
_____
_____
_____

SODAS Worksheet
Problem Solving

Date: _____ Written by: _____

Situation: _____

Option #1: _____

Disadvantages	Advantages
1	1
2	2
3	3

Option #2: _____

Disadvantages	Advantages
1	1
2	2
3	3

Option #3: _____

Disadvantages	Advantages
1	1
2	2
3	3

Solution: _____

_____

_____

Debrief / Notes: _____

_____

_____

_____

_____

_____

_____

_____

_____

_____

_____

_____

_____

_____

SODAS Worksheet
Problem Solving

Date: _____   Written by: _____

Situation: _____

Option #1: _____

Disadvantages	Advantages
1	1
2	2
3	3

Option #2: _____

Disadvantages	Advantages
1	1
2	2
3	3

Option #3: _____

Disadvantages	Advantages
1	1
2	2
3	3

Solution: _____
_____
_____

Debrief / Notes: _____
_____
_____
_____
_____
_____
_____
_____
_____
_____
_____
_____
_____

SODAS Worksheet

Problem Solving

Date: _____   Written by: _____

Situation: _____

Option #1: _____

Disadvantages	Advantages
1	1
2	2
3	3

Option #2: _____

Disadvantages	Advantages
1	1
2	2
3	3

Option #3: _____

Disadvantages	Advantages
1	1
2	2
3	3

Solution: _____

_____

_____

Debrief / Notes: _____

_____

_____

_____

_____

_____

_____

_____

_____

_____

_____

_____

SODAS Worksheet

Problem Solving

Date: _____   Written by: _____

Situation: _____

Option #1: _____

Disadvantages	Advantages
1	1
2	2
3	3

Option #2: _____

Disadvantages	Advantages
1	1
2	2
3	3

Option #3: _____

Disadvantages	Advantages
1	1
2	2
3	3

Solution: _____

_____

_____

Debrief / Notes: _____

_____

_____

_____

_____

_____

_____

_____

_____

_____

_____

_____

_____

SODAS Worksheet

Problem Solving

Date: _____   Written by: _____

Situation: _____

Option #1: _____

Disadvantages	Advantages
1	1
2	2
3	3

Option #2: _____

Disadvantages	Advantages
1	1
2	2
3	3

Option #3: _____

Disadvantages	Advantages
1	1
2	2
3	3

Solution: _____

_____

_____

Debrief / Notes: _____

_____

_____

_____

_____

_____

_____

_____

_____

_____

_____

_____

_____

_____

_____

_____

SODAS Worksheet
Problem Solving

Date: _____ Written by: _____

Situation: _____

Option #1: _____

Disadvantages	Advantages
1	1
2	2
3	3

Option #2: _____

Disadvantages	Advantages
1	1
2	2
3	3

Option #3: _____

Disadvantages	Advantages
1	1
2	2
3	3

Solution: _____
_____
_____

Debrief / Notes: _____
_____
_____
_____
_____
_____
_____
_____
_____
_____
_____
_____
_____
_____

SODAS Worksheet

Problem Solving

Date: _____ Written by: _____

Situation: _____

Option #1: _____

Disadvantages	Advantages
1	1
2	2
3	3

Option #2: _____

Disadvantages	Advantages
1	1
2	2
3	3

Option #3: _____

Disadvantages	Advantages
1	1
2	2
3	3

Solution: _____

_____

_____

Debrief / Notes: _____

_____

_____

_____

_____

_____

_____

_____

_____

_____

_____

_____

SODAS Worksheet
Problem Solving

Date: _____   Written by: _____

Situation: _____

Option #1: _____

Disadvantages	Advantages
1	1
2	2
3	3

Option #2: _____

Disadvantages	Advantages
1	1
2	2
3	3

Option #3: _____

Disadvantages	Advantages
1	1
2	2
3	3

Solution: _____
_____
_____

Debrief / Notes: _____
_____
_____
_____
_____
_____
_____
_____
_____
_____
_____
_____

SODAS Worksheet

Problem Solving

Date: _____ Written by: _____

Situation: _____

Option #1: _____

Disadvantages	Advantages
1	1
2	2
3	3

Option #2: _____

Disadvantages	Advantages
1	1
2	2
3	3

Option #3: _____

Disadvantages	Advantages
1	1
2	2
3	3

Solution: _____

_____

_____

Debrief / Notes: _____

_____

_____

_____

_____

_____

_____

_____

_____

_____

_____

_____

_____

SODAS Worksheet
Problem Solving

Date: _____   Written by: _____

Situation: _____

Option #1: _____

Disadvantages	Advantages
1	1
2	2
3	3

Option #2: _____

Disadvantages	Advantages
1	1
2	2
3	3

Option #3: _____

Disadvantages	Advantages
1	1
2	2
3	3

Solution: _____
_____
_____

Debrief / Notes: _____
_____
_____
_____
_____
_____
_____
_____
_____
_____
_____
_____
_____
_____

SODAS Worksheet

Problem Solving

Date: _____   Written by: _____

Situation: _____

Option #1: _____

Disadvantages	Advantages
1	1
2	2
3	3

Option #2: _____

Disadvantages	Advantages
1	1
2	2
3	3

Option #3: _____

Disadvantages	Advantages
1	1
2	2
3	3

Solution: _____
_____
_____

Debrief / Notes: _____
_____
_____
_____
_____
_____
_____
_____
_____
_____
_____
_____
_____

SODAS Worksheet

Problem Solving

Date: _____ Written by: _____

Situation: _____

Option #1: _____

Disadvantages	Advantages
1	1
2	2
3	3

Option #2: _____

Disadvantages	Advantages
1	1
2	2
3	3

Option #3: _____

Disadvantages	Advantages
1	1
2	2
3	3

Solution: _____

_____

_____

Debrief / Notes: _____

_____

_____

_____

_____

_____

_____

_____

_____

_____

_____

_____

_____

_____

_____

SODAS Worksheet

Problem Solving

Date: _____ Written by: _____

Situation: _____

Option #1: _____

Disadvantages	Advantages
1	1
2	2
3	3

Option #2: _____

Disadvantages	Advantages
1	1
2	2
3	3

Option #3: _____

Disadvantages	Advantages
1	1
2	2
3	3

Solution: _____

_____

_____

Debrief / Notes: _____

_____

_____

_____

_____

_____

_____

_____

_____

_____

_____

_____

SODAS Worksheet

Problem Solving

Date: _____   Written by: _____

Situation: _____

Option #1: _____

Disadvantages	Advantages
1	1
2	2
3	3

Option #2: _____

Disadvantages	Advantages
1	1
2	2
3	3

Option #3: _____

Disadvantages	Advantages
1	1
2	2
3	3

Solution: _____

_____

_____

Debrief / Notes: _____

_____

_____

_____

_____

_____

_____

_____

_____

_____

_____

_____

_____

SODAS Worksheet

Problem Solving

Date: _____   Written by: _____

Situation: _____

Option #1: _____

Disadvantages	Advantages
1	1
2	2
3	3

Option #2: _____

Disadvantages	Advantages
1	1
2	2
3	3

Option #3: _____

Disadvantages	Advantages
1	1
2	2
3	3

Solution: _____

_____

_____

Debrief / Notes: _____

_____

_____

_____

_____

_____

_____

_____

_____

_____

_____

_____

_____

SODAS Worksheet

Problem Solving

Date: _____   Written by: _____

Situation: _____

Option #1: _____

Disadvantages	Advantages
1	1
2	2
3	3

Option #2: _____

Disadvantages	Advantages
1	1
2	2
3	3

Option #3: _____

Disadvantages	Advantages
1	1
2	2
3	3

Solution: _____
_____
_____

Debrief / Notes: _____
_____
_____
_____
_____
_____
_____
_____
_____
_____
_____
_____
_____
_____

SODAS Worksheet
Problem Solving

Date: _____   Written by: _____

Situation: _____

Option #1: _____

Disadvantages	Advantages
1	1
2	2
3	3

Option #2: _____

Disadvantages	Advantages
1	1
2	2
3	3

Option #3: _____

Disadvantages	Advantages
1	1
2	2
3	3

Solution: _____
_____
_____

Debrief / Notes: _____
_____
_____
_____
_____
_____
_____
_____
_____
_____
_____
_____
_____
_____

SODAS Worksheet
Problem Solving

Date: _____ Written by: _____

Situation: _____

Option #1: _____

Disadvantages	Advantages
1	1
2	2
3	3

Option #2: _____

Disadvantages	Advantages
1	1
2	2
3	3

Option #3: _____

Disadvantages	Advantages
1	1
2	2
3	3

Solution: _____
_____
_____

Debrief / Notes: _____
_____
_____
_____
_____
_____
_____
_____
_____
_____
_____
_____
_____
_____

SODAS Worksheet
Problem Solving

Date: _____   Written by: _____

Situation: _____

Option #1: _____

Disadvantages	Advantages
1	1
2	2
3	3

Option #2: _____

Disadvantages	Advantages
1	1
2	2
3	3

Option #3: _____

Disadvantages	Advantages
1	1
2	2
3	3

Solution: _____
_____
_____

Debrief / Notes: _____
_____
_____
_____
_____
_____
_____
_____
_____
_____
_____
_____
_____
_____

SODAS Worksheet

Problem Solving

Date: _____ Written by: _____

Situation: _____

Option #1: _____

Disadvantages	Advantages
1	1
2	2
3	3

Option #2: _____

Disadvantages	Advantages
1	1
2	2
3	3

Option #3: _____

Disadvantages	Advantages
1	1
2	2
3	3

Solution: _____
_____
_____

Debrief / Notes: _____
_____
_____
_____
_____
_____
_____
_____
_____
_____
_____
_____
_____

SODAS Worksheet
Problem Solving

Date: _____   Written by: _____

Situation: _____

Option #1: _____

Disadvantages	Advantages
1	1
2	2
3	3

Option #2: _____

Disadvantages	Advantages
1	1
2	2
3	3

Option #3: _____

Disadvantages	Advantages
1	1
2	2
3	3

Solution: _____
_____
_____

Debrief / Notes: _____
_____
_____
_____
_____
_____
_____
_____
_____
_____
_____
_____
_____

SODAS Worksheet
Problem Solving

Date: _____   Written by: _____

Situation: _____

Option #1: _____

Disadvantages	Advantages
1	1
2	2
3	3

Option #2: _____

Disadvantages	Advantages
1	1
2	2
3	3

Option #3: _____

Disadvantages	Advantages
1	1
2	2
3	3

Solution: _____
_____
_____

Debrief / Notes: _____
_____
_____
_____
_____
_____
_____
_____
_____
_____
_____
_____

SODAS Worksheet

Problem Solving

Date: _____   Written by: _____

Situation: _____

Option #1: _____

Disadvantages	Advantages
1	1
2	2
3	3

Option #2: _____

Disadvantages	Advantages
1	1
2	2
3	3

Option #3: _____

Disadvantages	Advantages
1	1
2	2
3	3

Solution: _____
_____
_____
_____

Debrief / Notes: _____
_____
_____
_____
_____
_____
_____
_____
_____
_____
_____
_____

SODAS Worksheet
Problem Solving

Date: _____   Written by: _____

Situation: _____

Option #1: _____

Disadvantages	Advantages
1	1
2	2
3	3

Option #2: _____

Disadvantages	Advantages
1	1
2	2
3	3

Option #3: _____

Disadvantages	Advantages
1	1
2	2
3	3

Solution: _____
_____
_____

Debrief / Notes: _____
_____
_____
_____
_____
_____
_____
_____
_____
_____
_____
_____
_____
_____

SODAS Worksheet
Problem Solving

Date: _____   Written by: _____

Situation: _____

Option #1: _____

Disadvantages	Advantages
1	1
2	2
3	3

Option #2: _____

Disadvantages	Advantages
1	1
2	2
3	3

Option #3: _____

Disadvantages	Advantages
1	1
2	2
3	3

Solution: _____
_____
_____

Debrief / Notes: _____
_____
_____
_____
_____
_____
_____
_____
_____
_____
_____
_____
_____
_____

SODAS Worksheet

Problem Solving

Date: _____   Written by: _____

Situation: _____

Option #1: _____

Disadvantages	Advantages
1	1
2	2
3	3

Option #2: _____

Disadvantages	Advantages
1	1
2	2
3	3

Option #3: _____

Disadvantages	Advantages
1	1
2	2
3	3

Solution: _____

_____

_____

Debrief / Notes: _____

_____

_____

_____

_____

_____

_____

_____

_____

_____

_____

_____

_____

_____

_____

SODAS Worksheet

Problem Solving

Date: _____ Written by: _____

Situation: _____

Option #1: _____

Disadvantages	Advantages
1	1
2	2
3	3

Option #2: _____

Disadvantages	Advantages
1	1
2	2
3	3

Option #3: _____

Disadvantages	Advantages
1	1
2	2
3	3

Solution: _____
_____
_____

Debrief / Notes: _____
_____
_____
_____
_____
_____
_____
_____
_____
_____
_____
_____
_____
_____
_____

SODAS Worksheet
Problem Solving

Date: _____ Written by: _____

Situation: _____

Option #1: _____

Disadvantages	Advantages
1	1
2	2
3	3

Option #2: _____

Disadvantages	Advantages
1	1
2	2
3	3

Option #3: _____

Disadvantages	Advantages
1	1
2	2
3	3

Solution: _____

_____

_____

Debrief / Notes: _____

_____

_____

_____

_____

_____

_____

_____

_____

_____

_____

_____

_____

SODAS Worksheet
Problem Solving

Date: _____   Written by: _____

Situation: _____

Option #1: _____

Disadvantages	Advantages
1	1
2	2
3	3

Option #2: _____

Disadvantages	Advantages
1	1
2	2
3	3

Option #3: _____

Disadvantages	Advantages
1	1
2	2
3	3

Solution: _____

_____

_____

Debrief / Notes: _____

_____

_____

_____

_____

_____

_____

_____

_____

_____

_____

_____

_____

SODAS Worksheet

Problem Solving

Date: _____ Written by: _____

Situation: _____

Option #1: _____

Disadvantages	Advantages
1	1
2	2
3	3

Option #2: _____

Disadvantages	Advantages
1	1
2	2
3	3

Option #3: _____

Disadvantages	Advantages
1	1
2	2
3	3

Solution: _____

_____

_____

Debrief / Notes: _____

_____

_____

_____

_____

_____

_____

_____

_____

_____

_____

_____

_____

_____

SODAS Worksheet

Problem Solving

Date: _____ Written by: _____

Situation: _____

Option #1: _____

Disadvantages	Advantages
1	1
2	2
3	3

Option #2: _____

Disadvantages	Advantages
1	1
2	2
3	3

Option #3: _____

Disadvantages	Advantages
1	1
2	2
3	3

Solution: _____

_____

_____

Debrief / Notes: _____

_____

_____

_____

_____

_____

_____

_____

_____

_____

_____

_____

SODAS Worksheet

Problem Solving

Date: _____   Written by: _____

Situation: _____

Option #1: _____

Disadvantages	Advantages
1	1
2	2
3	3

Option #2: _____

Disadvantages	Advantages
1	1
2	2
3	3

Option #3: _____

Disadvantages	Advantages
1	1
2	2
3	3

Solution: _____
_____
_____

Debrief / Notes: _____
_____
_____
_____
_____
_____
_____
_____
_____
_____
_____
_____
_____

SODAS Worksheet

Problem Solving

Date: _____   Written by: _____

Situation: _____

Option #1: _____

Disadvantages	Advantages
1	1
2	2
3	3

Option #2: _____

Disadvantages	Advantages
1	1
2	2
3	3

Option #3: _____

Disadvantages	Advantages
1	1
2	2
3	3

Solution: _____
_____
_____

Debrief / Notes: _____
_____
_____
_____
_____
_____
_____
_____
_____
_____
_____
_____
_____

SODAS Worksheet

Problem Solving

Date: _____ Written by: _____

Situation: _____

Option #1: _____

Disadvantages	Advantages
1	1
2	2
3	3

Option #2: _____

Disadvantages	Advantages
1	1
2	2
3	3

Option #3: _____

Disadvantages	Advantages
1	1
2	2
3	3

Solution: _____
_____
_____

Debrief / Notes: _____
_____
_____
_____
_____
_____
_____
_____
_____
_____
_____
_____
_____

SODAS Worksheet

Problem Solving

Date: _____   Written by: _____

Situation: _____

Option #1: _____

Disadvantages	Advantages
1	1
2	2
3	3

Option #2: _____

Disadvantages	Advantages
1	1
2	2
3	3

Option #3: _____

Disadvantages	Advantages
1	1
2	2
3	3

Solution: _____

_____

_____

Debrief / Notes: _____

_____

_____

_____

_____

_____

_____

_____

_____

_____

_____

_____

_____

SODAS Worksheet

Problem Solving

Date: _____   Written by: _____

Situation: _____

Option #1: _____

Disadvantages	Advantages
1	1
2	2
3	3

Option #2: _____

Disadvantages	Advantages
1	1
2	2
3	3

Option #3: _____

Disadvantages	Advantages
1	1
2	2
3	3

Solution: _____

_____

_____

Debrief / Notes: _____

_____

_____

_____

_____

_____

_____

_____

_____

_____

_____

_____

_____

SODAS Worksheet

Problem Solving

Date: _____   Written by: _____

Situation: _____

Option #1: _____

Disadvantages	Advantages
1	1
2	2
3	3

Option #2: _____

Disadvantages	Advantages
1	1
2	2
3	3

Option #3: _____

Disadvantages	Advantages
1	1
2	2
3	3

Solution: _____
_____
_____

Debrief / Notes: _____
_____
_____
_____
_____
_____
_____
_____
_____
_____
_____
_____
_____
_____
_____

SODAS Worksheet
Problem Solving

Date: _____   Written by: _____

Situation: _____

Option #1: _____

Disadvantages	Advantages
1	1
2	2
3	3

Option #2: _____

Disadvantages	Advantages
1	1
2	2
3	3

Option #3: _____

Disadvantages	Advantages
1	1
2	2
3	3

Solution: _____
_____
_____
_____

Debrief / Notes: _____
_____
_____
_____
_____
_____
_____
_____
_____
_____
_____
_____
_____

About the Author

When it comes to parenting, Nicholeen Peck is a worldwide phenomenon and leader — and for good reason! Her proven system based on Four Simple Skills transforms even the most out-of-control teenagers and homes from chaos to calm within days. Though she's an international speaker, author, mentor, former foster parent of many difficult and troubled teens, and even President of the Worldwide Organization for Women (an approved consultant for the United Nations), Nicholeen spends most of her time at home with her husband and four children — which she knows will be her greatest impact and legacy. The fact that she has such an international influence while still being a stay-at-home mom is evidence of the effectiveness of her teachings. Learn more about her mission and methods at teachingselfgovernment.com.

RESOURCES TO IMPLEMENT
Teaching SELF-GOVERNMENT PRINCIPLES
IN YOUR HOME

If you want help implementing the Teaching Self-Government principles into your home, or would like more understanding of how it all works, then...

The Teaching Self-Government IMPLEMENTATION COURSE™ is just for you!

The Implementation Course includes:
- Advanced-level classes
- Video of actual parenting interactions
- Weekly group mentor calls with Nicholeen
- A special member forum for Q&A
- Ongoing support

Buy the full course at:
teachingselfgovernment.com/store

Also available at **teachingingselfgovernment.com**:
- Audio classes
- Family Tutorial DVD of the Aponte family learning Teaching Self-Government
- TSG Circle memberships
- TSG Weekly Support Group
- Children's books
- Cue Cards
- Poster of the Choices Map
- Books
- and more...

Made in the USA
Middletown, DE
26 October 2023

41433806R00124